The Curse of Tutankhamen

THE CURSE OF

TUTANKHAMEN

Elaine Landau

The Millbrook Press ❏ *Brookfield, Connecticut*
Mysteries of Science

Library of Congress Cataloging-in-Publication Data
Landau, Elaine.
The curse of Tutankhamen / Elaine Landau
   p.   cm. — (Mysteries of science)
Includes glossary of terms (p. 21-22).
Includes bibliographical references (p.   ) and index.
ISBN 0-7613-0014-7
   1. Tutankhamen, King of Egypt—Tomb—Juvenile literature.
   2. Egypt—Antiquities—Juvenile literature.   3. Blessing and
cursing—Egypt—Juvenile literature.   I. Title. II. Series: Landau
Elaine. Mysteries of science.
   DT87.5.L36 1996 932'.014—dc20   95-49092 CIP AC

Cover illustration and design by Anne Canevari Green

Published by The Millbrook Press, Inc.
2 Old New Milford Road, Brookfield, Connecticut 06804

Contents

For Michael

The Hidden Tomb

This story begins at another time in what may seem like another world. It's set thousands of years ago in ancient Egypt—a land of mystery and splendor in northeastern Africa.

As members of one of the earliest advanced civilizations, ancient Egyptians developed various forms of math, a 365-day calendar, and a system of picture writing known as hieroglyphics.

Talented Egyptian engineers, architects, and sculptors constructed wondrous cities as well. But perhaps their best known structures were huge stone pyramids built as tombs for their rulers.

Burial practices were extremely important to the ancient Egyptians. They believed in an afterlife (life after death) and saw dying as the gateway to their true and everlasting existence. To preserve an individual's body for eternal life they developed sophisticated techniques to embalm or mummify the corpse. As certain rituals were thought to smooth the path to eternity, a great deal of care also went into preparing the tomb. Usually burial chambers were filled with everything the person might need in the afterlife. This included food, clothing, cosmetics, jewelry, and furnishings among other items.

Rulers and wealthy Egyptians were often buried with statues of servants to wait on them in the next world. Prayers and spells from a text known as the Book of the Dead were painted on the tomb's walls. The ancient Egyptians believed these inscriptions would protect and guide the person in the afterlife.

Our book is about the discovery of the tomb of an Egyptian pharaoh named Tutankhamen who ruled more than 3,000 years ago. Tutankhamen was probably just nine or ten years old when he began his brief reign. Very little is known about the young pharaoh's background. He may have been of noble blood or a commoner. Some scholars think he could have been the son of Akhenaton, a former pharaoh, by one of his minor wives. Supposedly Tutankhamen bore a strong resemblance to Akhenaton. Yet it's also been suggested that Tutankhamen was adopted by the pharaoh and his queen, Nefertiti. Although the couple had a

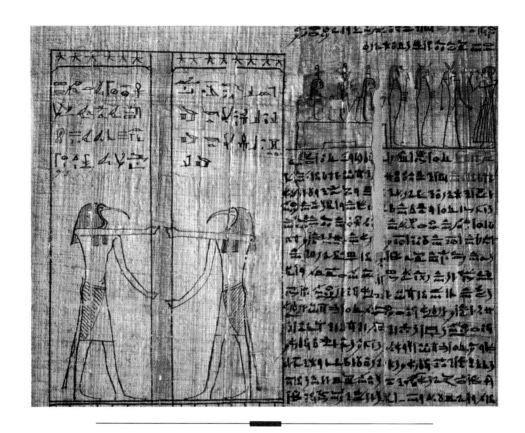

Ancient Egyptians were buried with collections of written material offering prayers and guidance for life after death. Frequently sections of these texts, known as The Book of the Dead, *were carved on the walls of their tombs.*

number of daughters, they never produced a male heir. In any case, Tutankhamen's claim to the throne was later strengthened by his marriage to Akhenaton's third daughter.

At first Akhenaton had selected his eldest daughter's husband to rule. But when both Akhenaton and his son-in-law died within two years of one another, Tutankhamen became next in line. Such child pharaohs were generally guided in affairs of state by court officials close to them. Tutankhamen's guide, or mentor, was a high-ranking court official named Ay. Ay arranged the young pharaoh's burial when Tutankhamen died at about eighteen years of age.

Much of Tutankhamen's short time as pharaoh was spent restoring Egypt to what it was before Akhenaton's rule. Akhenaton had proclaimed Aten (the sun god) as the only true deity, forcing people to abandon all of their other gods. He also moved Egypt's capital from Thebes to Akhetaton.

Encouraged by his advisers, Tutankhamen brought back the old religion, quelling some of the unrest Akhenaton had created. This greatly pleased the priests of the ancient faith as well as the general public, who tended to blame any misfortune or unpleasant occurrence on the wrath of the gods. Tutankhamen also moved the capital back to Thebes, where he enlarged and improved the temples of the old gods.

There have been many theories about how Tutankhamen died. Could his close advisor Ay, who became the next pharaoh, have grown tired of waiting? Or if the young ruler was truly of noble blood, could he have inherited the physical frailty that plagued many Egyptian royals of the time? Some scholars think he may have died from tuberculosis.

Though an examination of his mummy revealed no apparent signs of foul play, the actual cause of the young ruler's death may never be known.

Nevertheless, it's generally agreed that Tutankhamen's brief life and reign was hardly as spectacular as the discovery of his tomb by English archaeologist Howard Carter and his team. Their work was heralded as "a landmark in archaeological history" as well as "the most important single find in Egypt's Valley of the Kings" (a rocky desert area where numerous pharaohs are buried).[1]

Carter's November 26, 1922, discovery was especially noteworthy since the burial chamber of most pharaohs had been plundered by grave robbers, leaving little for archaeologists to find. But Tutankhamen was left largely undisturbed. That may be partly because Tutankhamen wasn't buried in a pyramid, making his final resting place more difficult for thieves to locate. Besides, for centuries Tutankhamen's grave remained well hidden from view by rock debris that had fallen from the nearby tomb of another pharaoh. Therefore grave robbers had only made several small openings in the walls of his tomb and removed just a few objects.

Admittedly, Tutankhamen's burial chambers were somewhat modest for a pharaoh. Some wonder if the young ruler had planned a more elaborate tomb for himself which wasn't completed at his time of death. Nevertheless, Carter's find thrilled archaeologists and Egyptologists (individuals

who study ancient Egypt) everywhere. It still yielded a magnificent array of ancient Egyptian artifacts and historical treasures.

Howard Carter described what he saw when he first held up a candle to look through a hole in the tomb's second doorway as ". . . strange animals, statues and gold, everywhere the glint of gold."[2] Filled with magnificent jewelry, furniture, and sculpture, the tomb contained everything a pharaoh would need in the afterlife. Since that time the splendid articles buried with Tutankhamen have been displayed at the Cairo Museum in Egypt as well as at various museums throughout the world. During the 1970s a traveling exhibition of Tutankhamen's effects was hailed as a major event in the art world.

Yet some say there may be a darker side to this landmark archaeological find—the "curse of Tutankhamen," a curse associated with the excavation that some feel serious scientists were too quick to dismiss. According to the legend, the trouble started when Howard Carter found an ordinary clay tablet covered with hieroglyphics in the tomb.

People usually think of the spectacular pyramids that surround Giza as the central burial site for the rulers of ancient Egypt, as indeed they were in about 2500 B.C. But from 1550 to around 1100 B.C., pharaohs were buried in underground chambers carved from rock on the west bank of the Nile, near Luxor. So many tombs have been discovered there, including Tutankhamen's, shown at left, that the area is known as the Valley of the Kings.

These are just two examples of the beautiful objects that caused
the drama and excitement of Carter's discovery to spread
beyond the world of archaeology and capture the imagination
of the general public. Above is a pendant depicting two
baboons in gold, lapis, and carnelian. At left is a detail
of a bed, with a lion's head made from wood and gold.

When the picture symbols were decoded, the tablet's inscription was said to have read:

Death shall slay with his wings
Whoever disturbs the peace of the pharaoh[3]

Some believers in the curse say that none of the archaeologists or scholars were concerned about the tablet. But expedition leaders supposedly feared that the native Egyptian laborers needed to pack and carry out the tomb's artifacts might be. Therefore, it's said that the clay tablet was purposely not listed along with the other items. Doubters point to the fact that the tablet also later conveniently disappeared from the site. But those who believe in the pharaoh's curse insist that the tablet was seen by numerous witnesses who never forgot its chilling message.

They further stress that another version of the curse was found when archaeologists explored the inner depths of Tutankhamen's tomb. This time the following warning was inscribed on the back of a statue:

It is I who drive back the robbers of the
tomb with the flames of the desert.
I am the protector of Tutankhamen's grave.

Some claim that a disturbingly strange series of events followed the tomb's opening. They say that within ten years after Tutankhamen's tomb was tampered with, nearly thirty people either directly or indirectly connected with the exca-

*As each object was removed from the tomb, it was placed on a stretcher
or tray and carried by a convoy of Egyptian workers and an armed
military escort to Carter's field laboratory at the end of the valley. Here
Carter is shown supervising the transport of a wooden life-size bust
of Tutankhamen. Some theorize that Carter suppressed all signs of
a curse on the tomb so that he would not lose his crew of workers.*

A KING'S SO-CALLED "CURSE"

The Tut-ankh-Amen Legend Is Again Revived

THE recent suicide of Lord Westbury has revived the superstition that a curse pursues all those who took part in the opening of King Tut-ankh-Amen's tomb. Lord Westbury, who jumped to his death from the seventh story of a building near Buckingham Palace, had been brooding over the death of his son, Richard Bethell, a member of the expedition which opened the Egyptian tomb. The coroner's jury ascribed Lord Westbury's death to his grief for his son, as well as to poor health. He was 78 years old.

Four days after the report of the suicide the newspapers contained this brief news item: "As a hearse and, because of his weakened condition, quickly proved fatal.

George Jay Gould was the second "victim." Out of curiosity he visited the Valley of the Kings, "forgetting that the Pharaoh's Ka (double) also wandered about that valley," as Dr. J. S. Madrus, the distinguished French Egyptologist and Orientalist, said. He caught a cold there which soon developed into an attack of pneumonia. The best doctors and the excavation to die. He had arranged with Howard Carter, who had assumed the leadership of the expedition after Lord Carnarvon's death, to make stereoscopic X-rays of the mummy Tut-ankh-Amen for the purpose of finding out how old the King had been when he died. This can be estimated in dead bodies by examining the juncture of certain bones and measuring the distance between them. Besides, he hoped to determine whether any jewels or ornaments were hidden beneath the thick, protective swathing of cloth with which the mummy was covered. But he never took the X-rays. About a month after the agreement was made he died in Switzerland.

As major newspapers began to use the term "curse," such as in The New York Times *headline above, increasing numbers of people began to wonder if Tutankhamen's curse was genuine.*

vation died suspiciously. These alarming stories dominated newspaper headlines around the world.

Yet skeptics argued that there still wasn't solid evidence to link the deaths to the archaeological dig. Did some individuals fascinated with ancient Egypt simply want to believe in the boy pharaoh's power from beyond the grave? Was there a strong profit motive involved as newspapers covering "the curse" reached record sales?

This book delves into this fascinating puzzle. As it reveals both sides of the story, you can decide for yourself whether or not Tutankhamen's revenge was real.

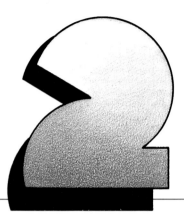

Legend or Truth

Among the deaths blamed on the curse of Tutankhamen was that of Lord Carnarvon, the English earl who largely financed the expedition.

Those who believe in the curse claim Carnarvon's illness began strangely. One morning the fifty-seven-year-old gentleman awoke shaking with chills and a temperature of over 104 degrees. The following day he seemed better, yet before long the high fever returned.

After that there was no real change in his condition for about two weeks.

Lord Carnarvon knew he was dying. During that period he told a friend, "I have heard the call, I am preparing."[1] Hearing that his father was gravely ill, Lord Carnarvon's son came to Cairo. During the night of his arrival he was awakened by the nurse, who told him that his father had died. He immediately went to his father's room, but at that moment all the lights suddenly went out. Lord Carnarvon's son recalled: "There was no explanation for the power failure all over Cairo. We asked the Cairo electric company, and they knew of no rational explanation for the lights going out and then on again."[2]

Carnarvon's son told of another curious incident connected to his father's death. He learned that thousands of miles away in London, England, the earl's fox terrier sat up on its hind legs and began to howl at the precise time of Lord Carnarvon's death. Then immediately afterward, the dog supposedly fell over dead.

Various reasons were given for Lord Carnarvon's demise. Cairo doctors believed that a shaving cut opened an old wound leading to the infection and fever. The earl's sister wrote that he died of blood poisoning due to a mosquito bite. Another theory was that he perished from pneumonia, which set in after an infection caused by the mosquito bite cleared up. Of course, others thought he was a victim of the curse of Tutankhamen.

It was rumored that the curse even extended to those who knew the tomb tamperers. George Jay Gould (son of

George Molyneux, Fifth Earl of Carnarvon (1866–1923), is sometimes credited as being the co-discoverer of Tutankhamen's tomb in that he not only financed Howard Carter's successful search, but also took an active role in the excavation.

the famous American financier Jay Gould) and a friend of the late Lord Carnarvon, visited the Valley of the Kings to see the boy pharaoh's tomb. But believers in the curse feel the trip was a fatal mistake. They claim that Gould awoke the next morning with a high fever and was dead by nightfall. Skeptics stress that several doctors noted that Gould had been ill for some time and was traveling in Egypt for his health. There were also rumors that Gould had bubonic plague while abroad. The precise cause of his death remains a mystery, causing some people to think that perhaps his demise was related to visiting the famous tomb his friend helped unearth.

Believers in the curse of Tutankhamen also insisted that it was responsible for the deaths of others linked to the excavation. These included American archaeologist Arthur Mace, who assisted in opening the tomb. Mace had supposedly pulled out the last stone blocking the entrance to the tomb's main chamber. Before long Mace began to feel weak and listless. Complaining of exhaustion, he was forced to sharply limit his activities. Unfortunately he fell into a deep coma from which he never awakened. Some said the forty-nine-year-old archaeologist had contracted tuberculosis before ever joining the Tutankhamen project. Others said that wasn't so. There are also those who think it may be more than a coincidence that Arthur Mace died in the same hotel as Lord Carnarvon.

Archaeologist Arthur Mace, standing at left, is shown outside of the tomb examining and applying a chemical treatment to an artifact that will be packed and transported to Carter's field laboratory.

Some stories of the deaths tied to the pharaoh's curse seemed especially bone-chilling. These include the death of Richard Bethell, Howard Carter's secretary on the Tutankhamen expedition. Believers in the curse of Tutankhamen argued that Bethell's demise set off a chain of unnatural occurrences. Grief stricken over his son's death, Bethell's seventy-eight-year-old father, Lord Westbury, committed suicide several months later. In describing the situation, a February 1930 Universal News Service report stated:

> Death of another distinguished person was linked to the curse of the pharaoh today when Lord Westbury committed suicide. Lord Westbury's son, Richard Bethell, acted as secretary to Howard Carter, when the latter supervised the opening of Tutankhamen's tomb. . . .
>
> The seventy eight year-old . . . took his life in a leap from the window of his seventh story apartment in the fashionable St. James Court, Westminster, crashing through a glass veranda and dying instantly as he struck the pavement.
>
> Lord Westbury had been worried about the death of his son, which occurred suddenly last November. Rumor attributed young Bethell's death to the superstition which declares that those who violate the tomb will come to a violent end.
>
> Lord Westbury was frequently heard to mutter, "the curse of the pharaohs" as though this had preyed on his mind. In a last letter he wrote: "I cannot stand the horror any longer and I am going to make my exit."[3]

Hearse With Lord Westbury's Body Kills Boy; Museum Death Also Laid to 'Pharaohs' Curse'

LONDON, Feb. 25 (Æ).—Two more deaths which the superstitious were inclined to associate with the opening of Tut-ankh-Amen's tomb were attracting attention here today.

As a hearse was bearing the body of the late Lord Westbury to a crematorium today, it knocked down and killed an 8-year-old boy, Joseph Greer. Lord Westbury had committed suicide on Saturday and his act was ascribed by many to the alleged curse of the Pharaohs. His son, Richard Bethell, died last November after serving as secretary to Howard Carter, who opened the tomb.

The other death was that of Edgar Steele, 57, a worker in the British Museum who had cared for some of the relics from the tombs of Luxor.

He died after an operation for an internal trouble.

An official of the museum scouted the suggestion that there was anything sinister in Steele's death, however, and Mr. Carter has declared that the curse is nothing but a myth.

The museum official remarked that thousands of people had been indirectly connected with the Tut-ankh-Amen relics and that there was no record of any overwhelming outbreak of mortality.

"I've handled Egyptian relics myself many times, for years, and I'm still as well as ever," he said.

The Pharaohs' curse, legend has it, doomed to a quick death any one molesting the tombs of the ancient Egyptian rulers.

This February 26, 1930 article from The New York Times *quotes a museum official as saying that thousands of people had been connected with Tut's relics without a problem — but the headline still cites the "pharaohs' curse."*

Believers in the curse point out that the tragic chain of events didn't end here. Sadly, the hearse carrying Lord Westbury's body to the cemetery ran over a little boy, killing the child.

Other seemingly questionable deaths linked to the curse included that of radiologist Archibald Reid, thought to be the first person to cut the binding on Tutankhamen's 3,000-

year-old mummy. This unraveling was necessary to X-ray the body. Yet according to curse believers, soon afterward Reid felt the exhaustion and fatigue experienced by some others who supposedly died as a result of the pharaoh's revenge. He was ill when he boarded the ship back to England, where he died.

Over a dozen other deceased professionals, including a number of educators and archaeologists who participated in opening and dismantling the tomb, were labeled victims of the curse as well. Although the press came up with fascinating accounts of their deaths, there were those who doubted these stories. Some suggested that to sell more newspapers, anyone who died who was even remotely connected to the expedition automatically became another of Tutankhamen's victims.

In some instances there appeared to be no real tie at all. This was especially evident in the murder of an Arab prince by his French wife while the couple stayed at a London hotel. Although newspapers claimed that the prince's end was due to Tutankhamen's curse, the prince had only briefly visited the tomb once while touring Egypt. Popular author and antiques collector Arthur Weigall was also described as a curse victim when he died. But although Weigall visited the tomb while in Egypt, he'd had nothing to do with the archaeological dig or anyone connected to it.

In other cases there were extremely varied reports of the deaths linked to Tutankhamen. For example, some sources cited radiologist Archibald Reid as having an active role in unwrapping and examining the pharaoh's remains. But other accounts said that while Reid had planned to X-ray the mummy, he died before arriving at the tomb. Numerous claims of the curse's far-reaching effect were difficult to believe.

A workman at the British Museum was supposedly labeling objects from Tutankhamen's tomb when he fell over dead. Yet after the story was published, it was learned that the Museum didn't have any such items at the time.

Skeptics stress that many individuals with major roles in the excavation remained in good health both during and after the project.

Howard Carter, who headed the expedition, died in 1939—sixteen years after uncovering Tutankhamen's tomb. The late Lord Carnarvon's daughter, Lady Evelyn Herbert, stood at her father's side as the tomb was explored. Yet she lived for almost fifty years afterward. Pierre Lacau, an Egyptologist involved in all phases of the project, died at ninety-two years of age. Another long-term survivor was anatomy expert Dr. Douglas Derry of Cairo University, who carefully examined the pharaoh's remains. He didn't die until he was well into his eighties, more than sixteen years after he'd worked on the mummy. Similarly Gustave Lefebvre, who organized the artifacts for permanent exhibition at the Cairo Museum, lived a full thirty-four years after the tomb was discovered.

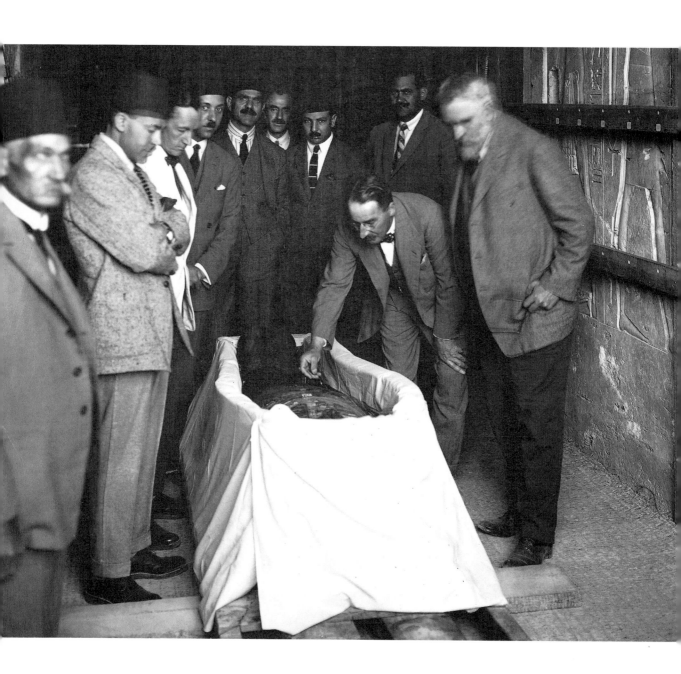

Yet those who still believe in the curse think these survivors were merely among those who escaped Tutankhamen's wrath. Some even insist that the curse was still active in the mid-1960s. They believe that the 1966 death of Mohammed Ibraham, Egypt's Director of Antiquities, is a prime example of the young pharaoh's revenge. The tragic events began when the Egyptian government first agreed to lend some Tutankhamen artifacts to a French museum for exhibition. Fearful of the curse, Ibraham argued against transferring the items. But he was eventually convinced by his superiors and the French ambassador to go along with the plan. Several days after he'd agreed, his daughter was seriously injured in an automobile accident. At about the same time, Mohammed Ibraham dreamed that he'd be involved in a life-threatening situation as well.

Feeling that the curse of Tutankhamen was at the root of the trouble, he tried to convince Cairo's minister of culture to cancel the exhibition. He also met with several French diplomats hoping to stop the museum loan. But

The dramatic moments in the unveiling of the tomb's wonders involved many individuals; trained professionals as well as government and institutional officials. Here a committee watches as Carter begins the process of unwrapping the mummy.

they convinced Ibraham that it was foolish not to share Tu-tankhamen's treasures with the world just because of a su-perstition.

Some think Mohammed Ibraham was gravely wrong to have ignored the curse. As he left the meeting with the French diplomats he was hit by a car and taken to the hospital with a fractured skull. He died two days later.

Other Explanations

Some individuals who don't believe in the
curse of Tutankhamen nevertheless feel
there may be still another mystery to unravel.

They think perhaps too many archaeologists
as well as others on these expeditions have
either become very ill or died.

Could their health problems somehow be
connected to their work?

That idea was first proposed by Dr. Ezzeddin Taha, a Cairo University doctor and biologist who held a press conference on November 3, 1962, to announce his theory. Dr. Taha had treated both archaeologists and various museum employees over the years. In examining individuals who worked in ancient Egyptian tombs, he noticed that many suffered from an unusual fungus.

Often these patients experienced high fever and inflammations of the upper respiratory system. Frequently there were also breathing problems as well as an itchy rash known as the "Coptic itch."

Through his research at Cairo University's Institute for Microbiology, Taha identified a number of disease-producing agents that could have affected these workers. One such fungus, known as *Aspergillus niger,* is exceptionally hardy. Scientists believe that it can survive for as long as four thousand years in mummies and burial tombs.

Could these disease agents be related to the medical problems blamed on the curse over the years? As Dr. Taha described his research and conclusions, "This discovery has once and for all destroyed the superstition that explorers who worked in ancient tombs died as the result of some kind of curse. They were victims of morbidia [deadly agents] encountered at work. Some people may still believe that the curse of the pharaohs can be attributed to [blamed on] some supernatural powers, but that belongs to the realm of fairy tales."[1]

Taha's theory may account for some of the deaths linked to Tutankhamen's revenge. But believers in the curse stress that many of those who died were involved in fatal accidents. Ironically, Ezzeddin Taha, who'd been active on archaeological expeditions himself, died in a car crash. He and two of his assistants were driving along the road when their car suddenly swerved and collided head-on with a vehicle coming from the opposite direction.

All three men in Taha's car died immediately. However, following an autopsy, doctors identified Taha's cause of death as circulatory collapse. Could that have been why he lost control of the car? Taha had believed that patients with the illness labeled "the pharaoh's curse" might be cured with the proper antibiotics. Since he worked with archaeologists and others who were possibly infected, he'd routinely taken antibiotics himself. But if his demise was due to such disease-producing agents, could his theory have been wrong? While some especially strong bacterial strains are resistant to antibiotics, there are no clear-cut answers in this case. But some feel that Dr. Taha's research and association with tomb tamperers made him a ripe target for Tutankhamen's revenge.

Over the years, other scientific explanations have been proposed to account for the deaths blamed on the curse. These include the theory that a number of deaths may have resulted from a poisonous parasitic hookworm commonly found in ancient tombs. Similar illnesses and deaths were frequently seen among European underground miners and tunnel builders who toiled in environments like those encountered by archaeologists. At one point the illness was so common among these groups that it was sometimes referred to as "tunnel disease."

In these cases, two poisonous glands near the hookworm's head release a deadly substance into the victim's body. Blood vessels carry the toxin to the person's circulatory system, where it destroys the red corpuscles, causing exhaustion, high fever, and sometimes death. Archaeologists, scientists, and laborers who spent extended periods in underground tombs were likely to have come in contact with a variety of parasites.

Still another explanation for the deaths may be that something stronger than an ancient curse was at work. It's well known that many ancient Egyptian high priests, court officials, and magicians were experts at producing potent poisons. In fact, high priests often cultivated small gardens of poisonous plants, which were used when necessary.

This is the west side of the antechamber as Howard Carter first viewed it. Could a sinister virus, a poison gas, or a nest of parasitic hookworms be concealed here?

Historians further indicate that the ancient Egyptians also made use of insect and animal poisons if it suited their needs. Poison from a scorpion common to the area was extremely deadly. The symptoms exhibited prior to death included muscle cramps, paralysis, a weak pulse, and labored breathing. Powerful poisons were also extracted from the glands of various snakes and spiders. Depending on the poison used, such substances either paralyzed the central nervous system or caused fatal blood clots to form. Deadly toxins taken from some types of dried beetles caused severe stomach cramps and mental disorientation if swallowed. A large enough dose could also result in circulatory paralysis and death.

High priests and court officials often played an essential role in planning and carrying out the burial of Egypt's rulers. As pharaohs were extremely concerned about grave robbers locating their tombs, it's been suggested that deadly poisons may have been used as a way to stop thieves.

Not much is known about how ancient Egyptian poisons were used because these carefully guarded secrets were passed down to only a select few. However, an intruder into a tomb wouldn't necessarily have to swallow a potion to be affected. Some suspect that powerful poisons used to paint tomb walls and artifacts only needed to penetrate the skin. Grave robbers, archaeologists, and laborers might easily have been affected as they physically examined the premises. Since some poisons may even be absorbed through natural

Did ancient Egyptian priests come up with ways of punishing those who would disturb the tombs of their pharaohs, even centuries later?

perspiration, anyone sweating within the warm confines of a tomb could have been stricken as well.

Possibly some of the poisons employed were actually lethal forms of bacteria capable of causing serious illness or death. Bacteria generally lose strength when exposed to air, light, and sun, but the dark, dank environment of the tightly vaulted ancient Egyptian tombs provided an ideal breeding ground for numerous lethal germs. The deadly bacteria might even have been nourished by the decomposing fats and oils on the mummy. Under these conditions some bacterial forms could retain their potency for centuries.

Certain types of decomposing bacteria also produce lethal vapors or gases that could possibly affect someone entering these airtight tombs. In such instances, the person had only to inhale for a deadly effect to take place. Unknowing archaeologists, scholars, and laborers who spent prolonged periods in the tombs never wore gas masks. Most ancient tombs, including Tutankhamen's, were discovered with holes about the size of an arm drilled in them. As this opening was too small to remove larger valuables, the hole might have been created by grave robbers to allow deadly vapors to seep out.

Yet if various forms of poison and deadly bacteria, rather than a pharaoh's curse, were the problem, why didn't *everyone* exposed either die or become gravely ill? Some argue that archaeologists who spent much of their lives in the tombs exposed to small amounts of these substances could

The "curse of Tutankhamen" did not seem to bother New Yorkers. When the tomb's treasures were brought to the Metropolitan Museum of Art in 1978, the ticket line for the exhibit was so long that street musicians gathered to entertain the crowds.

have built up a resistance over the years. Although they might experience some symptoms, they probably wouldn't even connect feeling sick with having spent months unearthing a tomb or similar site. Although Howard Carter was supposedly unaffected by "Tutankhamen's curse," some say he experienced bouts of dizziness and weakness, severe headaches, and even hallucinations. Could his discomfort have resulted from his work environment?

In the end, we are left with more questions than clear answers. Is "the curse of Tutankhamen" a myth or an unresolved mystery? Was the rash of deaths linked to it caused by ancient poisons or deadly bacteria? Or have the numbers of deaths merely been greatly exaggerated?

Lord Carnarvon's son and daughter did not believe in Tutankhamen's revenge. Yet due to their father's role in the expedition, they were often asked about it over the years. When interviewed, both denied that a curse existed and instead stressed the valuable archaeological finds resulting from the excavation. Nevertheless, some found Carnarvon's son's reply interesting when he was asked whether he would re-visit Tutankhamen's tomb. The sixth earl of Carnarvon simply declared: "Not for a million pounds!"[2]

Notes

Chapter One

1. Howard Carter, *The Tomb of Tutankhamen* (New York: E.P. Dutton & Co., 1954) p. 1.
2. I.E.S. Edwards, *Tutankhamen: His Tomb and Its Treasures* (New York: The Metropolitan Museum of Art and Alfred A. Knopf, Inc., 1976) p. 20.
3. Philipp Vandenberg, *The Curse of the Pharaohs* (New York: J.B. Lippincott, 1975) p. 21.

Chapter Two

1. Howard Carter and A.C. Moore, *The Discovery of the Tomb of Tutankhamen* (New York: Dover Publications, 1977) p. 39.
2. Philipp Vandenberg, *The Curse of the Pharaohs* (New York: J.B. Lippincott, 1975) p. 27.
3. Barry Wynne, *Behind the Mask of Tutankhamen* (Douglass, Wyoming: TAP Publishing Company, 1973) p. 198.

Chapter Three

1. Philipp Vandenberg, *The Curse of the Pharaohs* (New York: J.B. Lippincott, 1975) p. 170.
2. Barry Wynne, *Behind the Mask of Tutankhamen* (Douglass, Wyoming: TAP Publishing Company, 1973) p. 200.

Glossary

anatomy—the study of the inner structures of a person, animal, or plant

antibiotics—chemical substances used to inhibit or destroy bacteria. Antibiotics are often used to treat infectious diseases

archaeologist—a person who studies ancient cultures by examining remains (utensils, tools, art, etc.) chiefly discovered through excavation

artifact—any object made by human workmanship

autopsy—an examination of a deceased human

bacteria—microscopic organisms that can either be beneficial or harmful

Egyptologist—a specialist in the study of ancient Egypt

excavation—uncovering past civilizations by digging up their remains

hallucination—seeing or hearing something that isn't there

hieroglyphics—an ancient Egyptian writing system using pictures and symbols

hookworm—parasitic worm that lives on or in humans and animals

lethal—deadly

paralysis—a partial or complete loss of the ability to move a part of the body

pharaoh—a name given to the rulers of ancient Egypt

pyramid—a square-based structure with four triangular sides meeting at top

radiologist—a specialist in the interpretation and use of X-rays

scorpion—a small animal with a poisonous stinger at the tip of its tail

superstition—a belief contrary to the laws of science

toxin—a poisonous substance

Further Reading

Bendick, Jeanne. *Egyptian Tombs*. New York: Franklin Watts, 1989.

Berrill, Margaret. *Mummies, Masks & Mourners*. New York: Lodestar, 1990.

Biesty, Stephen. *Exploring the Past*. San Diego: Harcourt Brace Jovanovich, 1989.

Clare, John D., ed. *Pyramids of Ancient Egypt*. San Diego: Harcourt Brace Jovanovich, 1992.

Cohen, Daniel. *Ancient Egypt*. New York: Doubleday, 1989.

Coil, Suzanne M. *Poisonous Plants*. New York: Franklin Watts, 1991.

Croshen, Judith. *Ancient Egypt*. New York: Viking, 1993.

Giblin, James. *The Riddle of the Rosetta Stone*. New York: Harper, 1992.

Hart, George. *Ancient Egypt*. New York: Knopf, 1990.

Morley, Jacqueline. *An Egyptian Pyramid*. New York: P. Bendrick, 1991.

Nicholson, Robert. *Ancient Egypt*. New York: Chelsea Juniors, 1994.

Perl, Lila. *Mummies, Tombs, and Treasure*. Boston: Clarion Books, 1987.

Putnam, James. *Mummy*. New York: Knopf, 1993.

Putnam, James. *Pyramid*. New York: Knopf, 1994.

Reeves, Nicholas. *Into the Mummy's Tombs*. New York: Scholastic, 1992.

Roehrig, Catherine. *Fun With Hieroglyphics*. New York: Viking, 1990.

Terzi, Marinella. *The Land of the Pharaohs*. Chicago: Childrens Press, 1992.

Wilcox, Charlotte. *Mummies & Their Mysteries*. Minneapolis: Carolrhoda Books, 1993.

Index

About the Author

Elaine Landau has written more than eighty-five nonfiction books for young people and especially enjoys researching new topics.

While she was writing this book, her preschool-aged son developed an interest in mummies. He tightly wrapped a teddy bear in bandages and claimed to be waiting for a famous historian to uncover the "mummified" body. As far as anyone knows, he is still waiting.

Ms. Landau resides in Sparta, New Jersey, with her husband, son, and the bandaged bear.